THE AMBITIOUS PROFESSIONAL'S GUIDE TO
SURPLUS

THE AMBITIOUS PROFESSIONAL'S GUIDE TO
SURPLUS

- FIRST EDITION -

By: John Patterson & Kirkland Tibbels

Artwork and Design by: Paul Rossney

© 2021 Influence Ecology, LLC.

ISBN: 9798588091091

All rights reserved. Printed in the United States of America. No part of this book may be reproduced or transmitted in any form or by any means whatsoever without express written permission from the author, except in the case of brief quotations embodied in critical articles and reviews. Please refer all pertinent questions to the publisher.

Influence Ecology books are available through the publisher.
For more information, please write to:
Influence Ecology, LLC,
1000 Town Center Dr. Ste 300, Oxnard, CA 93036 USA.

www.influenceecology.com

BUSINESS PROFESSIONAL'S NAME

_____

TRANSACTIONAL PERSONALITY

_____

LOCATION (CITY & COUNTRY)

_____

GUIDE START DATE

_____

PHONE NUMBER

_____

Table of Contents

Chapter One
 Orienteering   15

Chapter Two
 The Goal of the Year of Surplus
  Why Do All This?   17
  What is Surplus?   17
  Why Does It Matter?   17
  Surplus and Satisfaction   17
  The Primary Breakdowns to Surplus   18
  The Ever-Elusive Having   18
  Mind the Duality Gap   18

Chapter Three
 Four Thresholds of Fitness
  Thresholds of Fitness   19
  Monthly Checkpoints   20

Chapter Four
 The First Threshold
 Know Thy Aims
 Month 1
  Conditions of Life™   23
  The Conditions of Life™   24
  What is Satisfaction?   25
  Accurate Thinking   26
  Inventory Your Life-Long Aims   27
  Your Aims Are Your Aims   29
  Yet to Emerge Aims   29
  Group Work   30
  Inventory Threats   31
  Get Help: The Interview   32
  Interview Questions to Consider Asking   32

Notes	33
Achievement Award Badges	35

Chapter Five
Month 2

2011 Theme of the Year: Focus	37
Focus Your Aim	38
Inventory Your Aims: This Year	39
Focus Your Environment	42
An Inquiry About Your Environment of Focus	42
Focus Your Study	43
An Inquiry About Your Study Focus	43
Notes	44
Achievement Award Badges	45

Chapter Six
Month 3

2012 Theme of The Year: Concentration	47
Concentration Inquiry	48
Concentration in Action	49
An Inquiry About Saying 'No'	49
Willingness to Decline	50
Check Where you Don't Respect Your Own Offer	51
Notes	52
Achievement Award Badges	53

Chapter Seven
The Second Threshold
Maintain Through Others

What is Maintenance?	56
Maintenance and the Conditions of Life™	57
Inventory: Aims Maintenance	58
Group Work	61
Get Help: The Interview	62
Interview Questions to Consider Asking	62
Notes	63

Chapter Eight
Month 4
2013 Theme of the Year: Cooperation	65
Willingly Working With Others	66
Check Where Any Are True	67
Additional Inquiry	68
Achievement Award Badges	69

Chapter Nine
Month 5
2014 Theme of the Year: Environment	71
An Aspect, Not an Entity	72
Produce the Required Environment	72
Additional Inquiry	73
Notes	74
Achievement Award Badge	75

Chapter Ten
Month 6
2015 Theme of the Year: Work	77
The Human Condition	78
Read the Human Condition	78
Notes	79
Achievement Award Badge	81

Chapter Eleven
The Third Threshold
Mind the Duality Gap
The Duality Gap?	84
The Gap Might Be Bigger Than Imagined	85
Rate Your Fitness Gap	86
Your Fitness Gap	87

Chapter Twelve
Month 7

2016 Theme of the Year: Sociality	89
Group Living	90
Group Work	91
Notes	92
Achievement Award Badges	93

Chapter Thirteen
Month 8

2017 Theme of the Year: Money	95
Money is a Tool	96
An Offer a Day	97
Notes	98
Achievement Award Badges	99

Chapter Fourteen
Month 9

2018 Theme of the Year: Career	101
Our Marketplace Identity	102
The Condition of Your Career	103
Group Work	104
Notes	106
Achievement Award Badges	107

Chapter Fifteen
The Fourth Threshold
Befriend Boredom

Boredom Begets Surplus	110
Gateway Concerns	111
Why Befriend Boredom?	111
Boredom: A New Problem to Befriend	112
What are our Aims in Surplus	112
Inventory Our Surplus Aims	113

Chapter Sixteen
Month 10
    2019 Theme of the Year: Ambition   117
    An Ambitious State of Mind   118
    Group Work   119
    Notes   120
    Achievement Award Badges   121

Chapter Seventeen
Month 11
    2020 Theme of the Year: Satisfaction   123
    Inventory Your Ten-Year Aims   124
    Why Ten-Year Aims?   126
    Notes   127
    Achievement Award Badges   129

Chapter Eighteen
Month 12
    2021 Theme of the Year: Surplus   131
    What did you discover on this journey?   132
    Achievement Award Badges   133

About Influence Ecology   135

THE AMBITIOUS PROFESSIONAL'S GUIDE TO SURPLUS

- CHAPTER ONE -
ORIENTEERING

The Ambitious Professional's Guide to Surplus offers a year-long journey to navigate from point to point in diverse and sometimes unfamiliar terrain while moving at speed. It can move you and your study groups through thresholds of fitness for surplus. You can conquer hurdles, steer clear of danger, and track milestones along the way.

The guide will not only introduce new concepts and principles but also will help establish potent new practices and habits. These include checklists, inventories, and provocative questions - all supported by individual and group activities, check-points, and more.

CHAPTER TWO
THE GOAL OF THE YEAR OF SURPLUS

Why Do All This?

We need surplus to thrive. While mere satisfaction may seem elusive to some, we must consider building surplus across many Conditions of Life™ to stave off the threats that will indeed happen. Threats are inescapable. For example, when our health is jeopardized, many of the Conditions of Life become vulnerable. It is easy to see how quickly we could endanger our career, money, relationships, and more.

What is Surplus?

Sufficient Help to Forestall Threats

Why Does it Matter?

Threats are unavoidable. During our Fundamentals of Transaction Program, we teach that "autonomy is not a state of self-reliance or independence but rather a state of having more help than you need." Freedom, certainty, consistency, and security are built with a surplus of valuable help...an ecology of valuable help.

Surplus and Satisfaction

How do these go hand-in-hand? True satisfaction is in the doing. If the doing "will do", chances are you're happy. Many of our most advanced students have developed fitness for some surplus and are now dealing with the breakdown of keeping what they've acquired. For most of us, however, we have discovered some naivety about the fitness required to satisfy our aims but can also see a gap in maintaining reproducible, whole-life satisfaction.

The primary breakdowns to surplus:

- We are aimless
- We are naive to maintenance
- Some Conditions of Life™ are threatened
- Our surplus isn't maintained through other people
- We don't have a surplus of influence
- We can't define or measure our satisfaction
- We don't know how to have
- We deplete our surplus
- We are naive to the gap of duality

The Ever-Elusive Having

Why is it most people don't know how to have? For example, we build a stash of cash then blow it. For surplus, we must know how to have.

Mind the Duality Gap

Are we naive to whole systems? The gap of duality is the gap created by one's inability to account for whole systems. For example, there is no real separation of mind and body, but dualistically, we sometimes think and behave as if these are separate elements. We threaten our satisfaction and surplus wherever and whenever we think and act as if elements of a whole are separate and distinct.

This gap can easily occur when we don't embody the framework of Transactional Competence™; when we can't think, act, and behave according to the transactional narratives, transactional behavior, or the true nature of ecologies.

As such, rather than trans-action, our activity devolves into self-action or inter-action.

FOUR THRESHOLDS OF FITNESS

- CHAPTER THREE -
FOUR THRESHOLDS OF FITNESS

Thresholds of Fitness

Upon examination, we may not be fit for surplus (a surplus of health, money, and other Conditions of Life). So what must we consider about our fitness so that surplus does not continue to elude us?

Fitness is the quality of being suitable to fulfill a particular role, task, or transaction; an ability to survive, succeed and thrive in a particular environment or condition. The Ambitious Professional's Guide to Surplus is structured to move you through thresholds of fitness organized by one year's quarters.

The First Threshold: **Know Thy Aims**

The Second Threshold: **Maintain Through Others**

The Third Threshold: **Mind the Duality Gap**

The Fourth Threshold: **Befriend Boredom**

• •

TIP: Slow Down to Speed Up

Fitness requires the time to develop one's competence by validating and modifying one's assumptions through repetitive action.

Don't cheat yourself out of the fitness required for sustainable surplus by looking for quick fixes. There aren't any.

THE AMBITIOUS PROFESSIONAL'S GUIDE TO SURPLUS

Monthly Check-Points

In addition, the guide offers monthly markers or check-points along the way. Each month, we'll offer guided activities informed by the *four thresholds of fitness* and the Influence Ecology themes of the last eleven years.

The first *month* is a full orientation. The first *theme*, Focus, begins on month two.

2011 Focus
2012 Concentration
2013 Cooperation
2014 Environment
2015 Activity
2016 Sociality
2017 Money
2018 Career
2019 Ambition
2020 Satisfaction
2021 Surplus

• • • • • • • • • • ● ● ● ● ● ● ● ● ● ● • • • • •

Earn Badges Along the Way

As you complete each month's activities, you can earn badges along the way. Track your progress

- CHAPTER FOUR -
THE FIRST THRESHOLD

KNOW THY AIMS

MONTH 1 | CONDITIONS OF LIFE™

MONTH 1

> "If you don't know where you're going, every road will get you nowhere."
> Henry A. Kissinger

Conditions of Life™

It all starts with thinking accurately about our aims in each Condition of Life.

We only transact to satisfy our Conditions of Life. Do we transact powerfully?

All of humanity is involved in reciprocal, consequential exchanges to satisfy our Conditions of Life. A Condition of Life is a circumstance, state, or situation that adults must tend to live a happy life. One can ignore these conditions, but ignoring them doesn't mean they don't exist. Some conditions become more or less important or relevant as a human being progresses through stages of living and aging.

If the most fundamental of these conditions is left unattended, the consequences produce a life of difficulty and hardship. Consistently unattainable satisfaction devolves into hopelessness, despair, and magical thinking.

The intent of this guide is to offer a metamorphic journey from one of non-reproducible success to holistic, whole-life satisfaction.

The Conditions of Life™

You need to understand what these conditions mean and how they are relevant to your satisfaction and surplus. Take time to read and study each. Look up words in a dictionary, discuss them with others.

1. **Health** – the condition of our biology
2. **Activity** – the labor, work, and action of life – what we do with our mind/body
3. **Knowing** – the condition of our ability to organize acts
4. **Relationship** – the condition of our ability and capacity to give and accept care and love
5. **Career** – the condition of our identity of value and help in specific ecologies
6. **Sociality** – the condition of our ability to function among others
7. **Money** – the condition of our capacity for meaningful economic exchange
8. **Ethics** – the condition of our character
9. **Education** – the condition of our specialized knowledge
10. **Fitness** - the condition of our being "fitted" for a satisfying life
11. **Aesthetics** - the condition of our appreciation of beauty and leisure
12. **Environment** - the condition of our world
13. **Politics** - the condition of cooperation and redistribution of resources
14. **Legacy** - the condition of our contribution of help to others
15. **Self-actualization/spirituality** - the condition of unconditionality

MONTH 1 | CONDITIONS OF LIFE™

What is Satisfaction?

What exactly is satisfaction in each Condition of Life?

First, you think accurately about each Condition. Then, you state your aim.

How would you know that you're satisfied? If you don't know, you can't be happy. If you don't know your aim, you can't be happy; you can't be satisfied.

A good question to ask yourself is "*will it do?*" (at reasonable cost or maintenance).

For example, will the aim I have and am successfully working to accomplish (e.g., retiring at age 60 with 4 million dollars) satisfy me? Does the activity to accomplish this aim satisfy me? Can I satisfy this aim at a reasonable cost to other Conditions of Life?

TIP: If You Mean It, Measure It.

Satisfaction is measured. In any transaction, the result of labor, work, and action is a measurable consequence.

What is your measure of satisfaction in each condition? What are the satisfaction metrics you must track to stay on course?

Accurate Thinking

Accurate thinking involves two fundamentals. First, you must separate facts from mere information. Second, you must separate facts into two classes, the relevant and the irrelevant.

How might you think accurately about any one of the Conditions of Life? Where might you be naive? For each condition below, write the name of one person who might help you think more accurately about that condition.

1. Health
2. Activity
3. Knowing
4. Relationship
5. Career
6. Sociality
7. Money
8. Ethics
9. Education
10. Fitness
11. Aesthetics
12. Environment
13. Politics
14. Legacy
15. Self-actualization/spirituality

MONTH 1 | CONDITIONS OF LIFE™

Inventory Your Life-Long Aims

For each Condition of Life below, state your aim **in 7-words or less**. State these as **life-long aims** for each condition.

Health _____

_____

Activity _____

_____

Knowing _____

_____

Relationship _____

_____

Career _____

_____

THE AMBITIOUS PROFESSIONAL'S GUIDE TO SURPLUS

Sociality _____

_____

Money _____

_____

Ethics _____

_____

Education _____

_____

Fitness _____

_____

Aesthetics _____

_____

Environment _____

_____

Politics _____

_____

MONTH 1 | CONDITIONS OF LIFE™

Legacy _____

_____

Self-actualization/spirituality _____

_____

Your Aims Are Your Aims

It is almost impossible not to be influenced by others. In fact, most of our aims are born out of wants we never imagined but observed in others. Your satisfaction depends on your ability to think accurately about YOUR satisfaction. What will do - for you?

Yet to Emerge Aims

Some aims don't emerge until later in life or until you've satisfied the more biological or linguistic aims. Let it be.

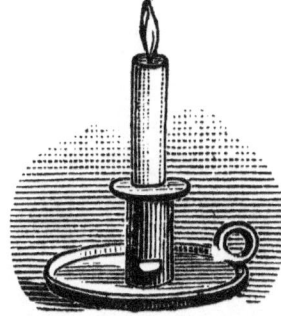

Did You Know?

It has been found that people can remember, on average, between five and nine digits or words at a time. When given seven numbers, most people could remember them and repeat them all.

Hint: You must remember your aims to transact for them.

Influence Ecology | 29

Group Work

With a study group, discuss your aims for **three or more** Conditions of Life. Ask each other the question, "will it do?" (at reasonable cost or maintenance). Be prepared to challenge yourself and others to think accurately about the aim, cost, or maintenance of each condition.

1. Health
2. Activity
3. Knowing
4. Relationship
5. Career
6. Sociality
7. Money
8. Ethics
9. Education
10. Fitness
11. Aesthetics
12. Environment
13. Politics
14. Legacy
15. Self-actualization/spirituality

MONTH 1 | CONDITIONS OF LIFE™

Inventory Threats

Check any threatened condition. Note the threat. Disregard any condition that has yet emerged as important or relevant.

- [ ] Health
- [ ] Activity
- [ ] Knowing
- [ ] Relationship
- [ ] Career
- [ ] Sociality
- [ ] Money
- [ ] Ethics
- [ ] Education
- [ ] Fitness
- [ ] Aesthetics
- [ ] Environment
- [ ] Politics
- [ ] Legacy
- [ ] Spirituality

Get Help: The Interview

Identify someone that has satisfied the Conditions of Life you seek to address. Invite them to be interviewed about those Conditions.

Interview questions to consider asking:

1. How did or do you satisfy that condition?
2. How do you maintain that condition?
3. How do you help those who help you?
4. What challenges did you overcome and how?
5. Where did you discover that you were naive?
6. If you were me, what would you do?
7. If you were me, what help would you get?
8. Where do you think I might be naive?
9. How do you think I might be in my own way?

Be prepared to hear feedback that may be difficult for you to hear. Some feedback may beget additional actions or it may even kill long-held dreams or prized ideas. Hint: this may be a good thing.

MONTH 1 | CONDITIONS OF LIFE™

Notes

THE AMBITIOUS PROFESSIONAL'S GUIDE TO SURPLUS

MONTH 1 | CONDITIONS OF LIFE™

Achievement Award Badges

MONTH 2 | 2011 THEME OF THE YEAR: FOCUS

- CHAPTER FIVE -
MONTH 2

"You don't get results by focusing on results. You get results by focusing on the actions that produce results."
Mike Hawkins

2011 Theme of The Year: Focus

Focus is the activity of singular deliberation; a central or single point, activity or attention.

Focus brings into view the specifics required to identify a subject.

Transactionally speaking, what we must 'bring into view' (and give identity to) is the specific labor, work, and action required to reach an end or aim.

What specific labor, work, and action can you bring into view and give identity to reach an aim?

What aim(s) require our focus?

THE AMBITIOUS PROFESSIONAL'S GUIDE TO SURPLUS

Focus Your Aim

Check the condition(s) which require your focus. Make any notes about this condition and what must be addressed.

- [ ] Health
- [ ] Activity
- [ ] Knowing
- [ ] Relationship
- [ ] Career
- [ ] Sociality
- [ ] Money
- [ ] Ethics
- [ ] Education
- [ ] Fitness
- [ ] Aesthetics
- [ ] Environment
- [ ] Politics
- [ ] Legacy
- [ ] Spirituality

MONTH 2 | 2011 THEME OF THE YEAR: FOCUS

Inventory Your Aims: This Year

For each Condition of Life below, state **a one-year aim** in **7-words or less**. Focus on this milestone during this year.

Health _____

_____

Activity _____

_____

Knowing _____

_____

Relationship _____

_____

Career _____

_____

THE AMBITIOUS PROFESSIONAL'S GUIDE TO SURPLUS

Sociality _____

_____

Money _____

_____

Ethics _____

_____

Education _____

_____

Fitness _____

_____

Aesthetics _____

_____

Environment _____

_____

Politics _____

_____

MONTH 2 | 2011 THEME OF THE YEAR: FOCUS

Legacy _____

_____

Self-actualization/spirituality _____

_____

_____

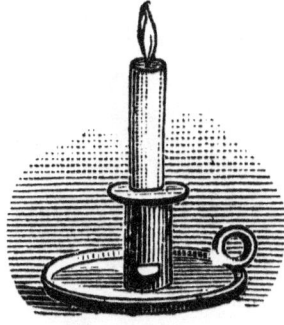

Did You Know?

It has been found that people tend to succeed when they create small milestones of success along the way. You can have an aim for your life, year, month, week - or even an aim for today.

Hint: Use milestones for obtainable victories.

Focus Your Environment

Your environment is often more powerful than your willpower. What changes do you need to make so that your environment helps you focus?

An Inquiry About Your Environment of Focus:

1. Where is the environment that requires your focus - and where should it be?
2. What might you add to your environment?
3. What might you remove?
4. What conversations need to be had with others so that you can focus?
5. What computer, phone, or tablet alarms, alerts, and click-bait must be turned on, off, or removed?
6. What objects might be added or removed?
7. How will this environment be maintained?

Make these changes to the environment and elicit the support of others.

MONTH 2 | 2011 THEME OF THE YEAR: FOCUS

Focus Your Study

To begin to satisfy this focused aim, what must you now study to support your ambition?

An Inquiry About Your Study Focus:

1. What is the general knowledge you must study? Who would know?

2. What is the specialized knowledge you must study? Who would know?

3. Name three people who could help you acquire the knowledge you need?

_____

_____

_____

How will you study this knowledge?

Schedule this focused study at a time where you can focus your attention. Did you schedule recurrent times?

Notes

MONTH 2 | 2011 THEME OF THE YEAR: FOCUS

Achievement Award Badges

2012 THEME OF THE YEAR: CONCENTRATION

- CHAPTER SIX -
MONTH 3

"Concentration is the secret of strength."
Ralph Waldo Emerson

2012 Theme of The Year: Concentration

We define concentration as an activity that increases the strength, force, or efficiency of something by removing any diluting element(s).

This important activity aims to create the proper situation and conditions that allow us to focus our mind and body on the work required to achieve specific results.

What is diluting your attention (to satisfying your aims or building surplus)?

What must you remove from your activity or environment?

THE AMBITIOUS PROFESSIONAL'S GUIDE TO SURPLUS

Concentration Inquiry

What must you concentrate (remove diluting elements)?

1. Where or how is your career identity diluted?
2. Where or how is the identity of your offer diluted?

We teach to offer solutions to substantial breakdowns in specific ecologies and for specific customers:

1. Where is your solution diluted?
2. Where is your breakdown diluted?
3. Where is your specific ecology/customer diluted?

_____

_____

_____

_____

_____

If this inquiry leads to new actions, make any changes and elicit the support of others.

2012 THEME OF THE YEAR: CONCENTRATION

Concentration in Action

What activity might you cease to concentrate?

This month, practice saying 'No' to invitations and requests that dilute your attention.

An Inquiry About Saying 'No':

1. What do you accept that dilutes your attention?

2. What do you accept that then requires maintenance?

3. With whom do you struggle most saying 'no'?

4. What practices could you invent that allow you to pause before you accept or decline?

5. Some find overwhelm and busyness a badge of honor and purpose; if this is true for you, what might honor you instead?

If this inquiry leads to new habits and practices, make any changes to the environment and elicit the support of others.

THE AMBITIOUS PROFESSIONAL'S GUIDE TO SURPLUS

Willingness to Decline

Ambitious adults are inundated with invitations, offers, and requests from others in every Condition of Life.

Staying present to your aims in each Condition of Life and being informed by the commitments, promises, and obligations already in place will be your greatest guide for what invitations, offers and requests will (or will not) offer you the best use of your time, energy, talent, and concerns.

> "If you don't respect your own offer, no one else will."
> Kirkland Tibbels

Powerful Identities & Declines: saying nothing is not the same thing as declining. Authority is built on what you decline. Remember, we are defined as much, if not more, by what we decline as we are by what we accept.

When people decline your invitations, offers, and requests—accept them powerfully and in the proper moods and attitudes that demonstrate your commitments and ethics.

2012 THEME OF THE YEAR: CONCENTRATION

Check Where You Might Not Respect Your Own Offer

- [ ] Your Time
- [ ] Your Value
- [ ] Your Labor, Work, or Activity
- [ ] Your Relationship
- [ ] Your Family
- [ ] Your Health
- [ ] Your Leisure
- [ ] Your Ethics
- [ ] Your Education
- [ ] Your Money

Remember, if you don't respect your own offer, no one will. It is likely that you are accepting rather than declining. If this is the case, discuss with your study group how you might practice the graceful decline; saying no with finess and gratitude.

THE AMBITIOUS PROFESSIONAL'S GUIDE TO SURPLUS

Notes

2012 THEME OF THE YEAR: CONCENTRATION

Achievement Award Badges

MAINTAIN THROUGH OTHERS

- CHAPTER SEVEN -
THE SECOND THRESHOLD

MAINTAIN THROUGH OTHERS

THE AMBITIOUS PROFESSIONAL'S GUIDE TO SURPLUS

What is Maintenance?

Maintenance is the activity of maintaining or preserving someone or something.

Four general types of maintenance approaches can be identified: corrective, preventive, risk-based, and condition-based maintenance.

- Corrective maintenance is aimed at fixing problems once they happen.
- Preventive maintenance is aimed at catching and fixing problems before they happen.
- Risk-based maintenance prioritizes maintenance resources toward assets that carry the most risk if they were to fail.
- Condition-based maintenance is when systems are carefully observed for changes that could indicate upcoming failure.

The cost of regular maintenance is minimal compared to the cost of a major breakdown; however, all maintenance has a cost. In fact, all transactions come with the labor, work, and action to maintain them.

Why do we rarely consider this cost, especially during the invention of new transactions?

To produce surplus (and free your resources for other concerns), consider where you can transact with others to maintain the activity on your behalf.

MAINTAIN THROUGH OTHERS

Maintenance and the Conditions of Life™
Review the Conditions of Life with maintenance in mind. How are these maintained? Who maintains them?

1. **Health** – the condition of our biology
2. **Activity** – the labor, work, and action of life – what we do with our mind/body
3. **Knowing** – the condition of our ability to organize acts
4. **Relationship** – the condition of our ability and capacity to give and accept care and love
5. **Career** – the condition of our identity of value and help in specific ecologies
6. **Sociality** – the condition of our ability to function among others
7. **Money** – the condition of our capacity for meaningful economic exchange
8. **Ethics** – the condition of our character
9. **Education** – the condition of our specialized knowledge
10. **Fitness** - the condition of our being "fitted" for a satisfying life
11. **Aesthetics** - the condition of our appreciation of beauty and leisure
12. **Environment** - the condition of our world
13. **Politics** - the condition of cooperation and redistribution of resources
14. **Legacy** - the condition of our contribution of help to others
15. **Self-actualization/spirituality** - the condition of unconditionality

THE AMBITIOUS PROFESSIONAL'S GUIDE TO SURPLUS

Inventory: Aims Maintenance

For each Condition of Life below, state how each is now maintained - or how it could be maintained.

Health _____

_____

Activity _____

_____

Knowing _____

_____

Relationship _____

_____

Career _____

_____

MAINTAIN THROUGH OTHERS

Sociality _____

_____

Money _____

_____

Ethics _____

_____

Education _____

_____

Fitness _____

_____

Aesthetics _____

_____

Environment _____

_____

Politics _____

_____

THE AMBITIOUS PROFESSIONAL'S GUIDE TO SURPLUS

Legacy _____

_____

Self-actualization/spirituality _____

_____

_____

• • • • • • • • • • ● ● ● ● ● ● ● ● ● ● • • • • • •

TIP: Others Want to Help

As you consider having some conditions maintained through others, remember that others may seek to satisfy their aims by offering the solution of maintenance to you!

Although maintenance may not sound fun to you, others find it valuable and satisfying.

MAINTAIN THROUGH OTHERS

Group Work

With a study group,
discuss how **three or more** Conditions of Life could be maintained through others. Be prepared to challenge yourself and others to think accurately about the transactions for maintenance for each condition.

1. Health
2. Activity
3. Knowing
4. Relationship
5. Career
6. Sociality
7. Money
8. Ethics
9. Education
10. Fitness
11. Aesthetics
12. Environment
13. Politics
14. Legacy
15. Self-actualization/spirituality

Get Help: The Interview

Identify someone that has satisfied the Conditions of Life you seek to address. Invite them to be interviewed about the maintenance of these Conditions.

Interview questions to consider asking:

1. How do you maintain that condition?
2. Does someone maintain this for you? How?
3. What is the exchange with others for this maintenance?
4. What challenges did you overcome to maintain this condition?
5. How do you consider maintenance on the front-end of transactions?

MAINTAIN THROUGH OTHERS

Notes

MONTH 4 | 2013 THEME OF THE YEAR: COOPERATION

- CHAPTER EIGHT -
MONTH 4

> "The only thing that will redeem mankind, is cooperation."
> Bertrand Russell

2013 Theme of The Year: Cooperation

The act of committing to and willingly working with others to produce the functions and results required to achieve specific aims.

A key phrase here is "willingly working with others" - note that it does not say "begrudgingly working with others." Rather than consider cooperation a necessary evil, consider it the only means to think and act in ways you'll never consider on your own.

Think of cooperation as a means to access a bigger brain. C.S. Lewis said, "Two heads are better than one." When two or more people work together, they are more likely to solve a problem than one person doing it alone.

Willingly Working with Others

Influence Ecology has studied over 220 personality models, the majority of which are based on a four-quadrant model.

Through most of human history, it has been posited that human beings generally fall into one of four basic personality or behavioral types or temperaments. The earliest record of this was written in 400BC by Hippocrates, who noted that the four basic temperaments of human behavior were:

Idea-Oriented
Theory-Oriented
Action-Oriented
Fact-Oriented

It is posited that we are a eusocial species* where different individuals have different jobs to do. There is a division of labor, generations overlap, occupy the same colony, and cooperate in caring for the young.

For example, an ant colony includes a Queen (reproduce), Workers (hunt/protect), Drones (mate), and Alates (establish new colonies).

While born genetically similar, environmental triggers evoke genetic switches to produce the perfect balance of the required roles.

Each role allows the collective group to thrive.

MONTH 4 | 2013 THEME OF THE YEAR: COOPERATION

Check Where Any Are True

You (or others) may suffer where any of the following are true. Once identified, discuss each with a study group to further understand your naivete and develop your fitness for cooperation.

- [ ] You rush to action rather than gain buy-in
- [ ] Life would turn out if others would go along with you
- [ ] I care so much that you should forgive my tardiness
- [ ] You'd prefer not to be obligated to tasks or meetings
- [ ] You would rather just do it yourself
- [ ] If not included, you get resentful
- [ ] Your standards are the way things should be done
- [ ] Without evidence, you're likely to say 'no'
- [ ] You are unaware of your cost to others
- [ ] In any meeting, you always try to contribute your input
- [ ] People should just deal with you the way I are
- [ ] You shouldn't have to compromise for others

THE AMBITIOUS PROFESSIONAL'S GUIDE TO SURPLUS

Additional Inquiry

1. What is the asset/liability of my personality?
2. What is the value/cost of my personality in a transaction?
3. What is the role or narrative I'm best fitted for in a transaction?
4. What personalities, roles, or narratives might I tend to avoid or dismiss?
5. How might I transact with other personalities?

MONTH 4 | 2013 THEME OF THE YEAR: COOPERATION

Achievement Award Badges

- CHAPTER NINE -
MONTH 5

> "Environment is stronger than will."
> Paramahansa Yogananda

2014 Theme of The Year: Environment

Environment is the aggregate of surrounding things; it is a channel or medium of activity.

You are an organism inseparable from environment.

Ecologies are complex, dynamic, adaptive systems.

Exchanges (transactions) are reciprocal and co-constitutive; both influence and reciprocally constitute one another.

An Ambitious Adult recognizes that an Ambitious State of Mind is an environmental phenomenon.

Are we naïve to the consequential environments we must occupy, produce, or maintain to satisfy our aims?

If we pay attention to environment, it makes a huge difference in how we perform.

An Aspect, Not an Entity

We are an aspect of the environments we occupy; we are not separate and distinct entities—however, that is not how we typically relate to the phenomenon. We tend to see ourselves as able to project our will onto objects, others, and whole environments. We tend to assume (naïvely) that we can force these others to obey our command, and in some cases, our requests devolve into demands, coercion, or outright combat.

Produce the Required Environment

We seed the targeted environment with the ideas, narratives, objects, and standards required to satisfy carefully articulated aims. An intuitive student will begin to see that ideas, narratives, processes, or standards are correlated with each personality. While the most objective-minded will easily see processes, structures, practices, measurements, standards, and regulations to bring back to their team, department, or function...they may not naturally see how to produce or maintain ideas, contexts, frameworks, relationships, stories, or missions.

Each personality might, therefore, be proficient (or fit) to build an influence ecology in ways that are obvious to them; but trapped in their own perspective they might be missing something that works against their aims. We can study the proficiencies of each personality to determine our own (or our team members') fitness to influence an ecology. We can then know where we're an asset and where we might need reinforcements from others.

MONTH 5 | 2014 THEME OF THE YEAR: ENVIRONMENT

Additional Inquiry

1. What is the proficiency of my personality? Select One

   Ideas
   Narratives
   Objects
   Standards

1. In the spaces below, describe your use of this proficiency.
2. How does my proficiency help occupy, build, or maintain the environment?
3. Where might I contribute this to the environment?
4. Where might I withhold this from the environment?

_____
_____
_____
_____
_____
_____

Notes

MONTH 5 | 2014 THEME OF THE YEAR: ENVIRONMENT

Achievement Award Badges

Influence Ecology | 75

MONTH 6 | 2015 THEME OF THE YEAR: WORK

- CHAPTER TEN -
MONTH 6

"Without labor nothing prospers."
Sophocles

2015 Theme of The Year: Activity

Activity is what we do with our mind and our body to take care of and cause our lives.

Activity is a constitutive aspect of all Conditions of Life; that is, activity is required to produce (bring into existence) and maintain the objects, conditions, and situations that constitute our living "in the world."

Many people tend to confuse the Work they do with the creation and production of Money. In other words, they only know Work as labor and use their mind and body in exchange for Money.

Without the proper orientation and understanding of the difference between Activity, Career, and Money, this unfortunate coupling can only produce limited prosperity.

THE AMBITIOUS PROFESSIONAL'S GUIDE TO SURPLUS

The Human Condition

The Human Condition, first published in 1958, is Hannah Arendt's account of how "human activities" should be and have been understood throughout Western history. Arendt is interested in the active life as contrasted with the contemplative life and concerned that the debate over the relative status of the two has blinded us to important insights about the active life and the way in which it has changed since ancient times. She distinguishes three sorts of activity (labor, work, and action) and discusses how they have been affected by changes in Western history.

Read the Human Condition

While not an easy read, we highly recommend that you acquire and read this book. The book (and summaries) can be found on the internet in a variety of forms.

MONTH 6 | 2015 THEME OF THE YEAR: WORK

Notes

THE AMBITIOUS PROFESSIONAL'S GUIDE TO SURPLUS

MONTH 6 | 2015 THEME OF THE YEAR: WORK

Achievement Award Badges

- CHAPTER ELEVEN -
THE THIRD THRESHOLD

MIND THE DUALITY GAP

The Duality Gap?

The duality gap is the gap created by one's inability to account for whole systems. For example, there is no real separation of mind and body, but we sometimes think and behave as if these aspects are distinct. We threaten our satisfaction and surplus wherever and whenever we think and act as if elements of a whole are separate and distinct.

This gap can occur when we don't embody the framework of Transactional Competence™: when we can't think, act, and behave according to the transactional narratives, transactional behavior, or the true nature of ecologies.

> "Viewed in its philosophical dimension, transaction denotes a reciprocal relationship between that which acts and that which is acted upon. In this relationship, both become united for the moment in a mutual transition or "transaction." It is a process in which both are reciprocally transformed. That is to say, the nature of the change each undergoes is affected by the presence and influence of the other. The relationship forms a bond of unity which contradicts any absolute separation or isolation which [...] is imposed by dualistic categories."
>
> Phillips, Trevor Joseph (2013). Transactionalism: An Historical and Interpretive Study.

Why this matters is simple: we are not separate and distinct entities, but rather aspects of whole ecosystems. For example, it is easy to see a child not account for the consequence of their actions on others, but can we identify the gap for ourselves?

MIND THE DUALITY GAP

The Gap Might Be Bigger Than Imagined

There is no absolute separation or isolation between you and the environments you occupy. You are the product of millions of years of evolutionary transactions, including the oxygen you breathe, your microbiome, and your sapien sociality.

Yet, we often think of ourselves as objects that overlord other objects or as individuals whose freedoms are inconsequential to others. We are keen to tout our merits; we are rather naive about our costs.

Transactional philosophy introduces concepts of action that illustrate the gap. For example, self-action is an activity that locates the individual as an overlord of all things, willing things to go your way. Inter-action is an activity that locates the individual as an object causing other objects to move, attempting to get things to go your way through force.

Trans-action properly orients us to the co-constitutive, reciprocal exchange with others and all things. A surplus of sociality, money, or identity (career) comes about when we correctly see ourselves as mere aspects of a larger whole.

This guide will by no means close a wide gap, for that, we recommend our advanced curriculum. However, you can begin to identify some trends that reveal more about this gap.

Note: Be as truthful to yourself as possible.

THE AMBITIOUS PROFESSIONAL'S GUIDE TO SURPLUS

Rate Your Fitness Gap

Rate yourself on a scale from 1 to 10 (10 being highest) on each of the following attributes. You can then total them for a sense of your fitness in this threshold.

- [ ] I empathize with other views, even when I disagree.
- [ ] I account for my cost to others in transactions
- [ ] I politely invite people to consider my views
- [ ] Others can easily follow my directions or instructions
- [ ] Those around me readily seek my input
- [ ] Rather than impose my will, I invite participation
- [ ] Rather than coerce, I seek a meeting of the minds
- [ ] I prefer to seek buy-in rather than seek forgiveness.
- [ ] I don't rely on manifestation from the uniiverse
- [ ] I know that the cosmos does not bend to my will
- [ ] If I need something done, I involve others
- [ ] Forcing others to act is not how I get things done
- [ ] I think about my social responsibility in most matters

MIND THE DUALITY GAP

Your Fitness Gap

Add up the totals and check your fitness gap.

102-130 Congratulations, you seem fit to move trans-actionally, accounting for co-constitutive, reciprocal exchanges with others and all things.

72-101 It is time to develop your fitness in some areas. While skilled, identify the lower ratings and inquire with others how you might improve.

42-71 You are struggling to transact powerfully and are instead self-acting or inter-acting. You'd rather not have to deal with people unless absolutely necessary. A surplus of sociality, money, or identity (career) comes about when we correctly see ourselves as mere aspects of a larger whole.

13-42 Said as politely as possible, you may be an a**hole, with little or no consideration for what it is like for others to transact with you.*

*You may want to read: Assholes: A Theory by Aaron James. What does it mean for someone to be an asshole? According to James, an asshole "allows himself to enjoy special advantages in social relations out of an entrenched sense of entitlement that immunizes him against the complaints of other people."

MONTH 7 | THEME OF THE YEAR: SOCIALITY

- CHAPTER TWELVE -
MONTH 7

"We are somehow natured not just to reproduce, but for sociality and even for culture."
Leon Kass

2016 Theme of The Year: Sociality

The condition of our ability and capacity to function among others.

THE AMBITIOUS PROFESSIONAL'S GUIDE TO SURPLUS

Group Living

Sociality means 'group living.' The formulation of any general theory of social behavior begins with a description of the selective forces causing and maintaining group living. In general, groups form and persist because all of the individuals involved somehow gain genetically.

Group living and cooperation is universally and automatically beneficial to all concerned and is a basic organizing, survival, and reciprocal attribute for many organisms. Human beings are social beings and live, work, and exist as such in groups.

This is a Condition of Life that is unavoidable and inescapable for an individual if they are to survive. Society is made up of groups or ecologies. Members belong to ecologies, and function in a defined capacity – roles. Individuals occupy and perform roles in social groups.

- Society is made up of groups or ecologies
- Members belong to ecologies, and function in a defined capacity - roles
- Individuals occupy and perform roles in social groups
- Roles are made up of organized practices
- A practice is a unit or set of organized reciprocal behaviors or acts

In the absence of a means to satisfy an aim, humankind concedes to:

1. Believe that something, somehow will make it better
2. Congregate with others who have similar desires
3. Toil in hopes our hard work will somehow pay off
4. Protest the way things are in lieu of any solutions

Each of the above are correlated to Transactional Behavior™.

MONTH 7 | THEME OF THE YEAR: SOCIALITY

Group Work

With a study group,
discuss how you might develop and practice the following. Be prepared to challenge yourself and others to think accurately.

1. Functioning (powerfully) among others
2. Transacting (competently) among others
3. Your role and it's correlated practices
4. Navigating an indifferent marketplace
5. Building offers of value
6. Understanding money and economic action

_____
_____
_____
_____
_____
_____

Notes

MONTH 7 | THEME OF THE YEAR: SOCIALITY

Achievement Award Badges

MONTH 8 | 2017 THEME OF THE YEAR: MONEY

- CHAPTER THIRTEEN -
MONTH 8

"The price of anything is the amount of life you exchange for it."
Henry David Thoreau

2017 Theme of The Year: Money

Money is a tool of meaningful exchange. Money is help.

THE AMBITIOUS PROFESSIONAL'S GUIDE TO SURPLUS

Money is a Tool

Money is the condition of our ability and capacity to function with others in meaningful economic exchange.

Our study will make it clear that money is a tool that offers us the ability to expand our abilities and capacities to transact socially in the exchange of objects to satisfy multiple Conditions of Life over a long period of time.

Money not only offers us the ability to exchange one thing for another in a way that expands our ability to get help and live a comfortable life, but it is also fulfilling and meaningful to be able to do so without making evident a particular sacrifice. It "means something" to us to be able to take care of and satisfy our needs in this way.

When we have little or no money, we must be concerned for and be sensitive to many situations and people that we would otherwise prefer to avoid or ignore. Money allows us to be indifferent to the concerns of others and offers us substantial freedom from the constraints and limits that we would suffer if not for its many benefits.

The more money we have in surplus, the more options, opportunities, indifference, and autonomy we enjoy. We will also touch on the power of "potentiality" that is available to people who demonstrate they have money in surplus.

Money is not easy to define beyond the common, everyday discourse. Money is often misunderstood as solely the form it takes, so we take great care in distinguishing money as help rather than simply an objective artifact. Money in all its forms and functions is help, which means not only the help it allows us to acquire but also what we must offer in order to exchange what we have for it.

Money is brought into our possession by means of exchange.

MONTH 8 | 2017 THEME OF THE YEAR: MONEY

An Offer a Day

During the month of Money, we advise the following practice:

Make one offer a day for 30 days.

To do this, there must be an offer by you, and an acceptance by another party, and an exchange of consideration (something of value). To do this each day, you'll have to invent offering something of value in exchange for something of value - and gain acceptance, decline, or counter offer.

This daily practice will develop your fitness for exchange. While it may be awkward at first, for monetary aims, we can not recommend it enough.

Use your study group to discuss the topic, practice, or get help inventing offers. Practice very simple offers and a few consequential offers.

· · · · · · · · · · ● ● ● ● ● ● ● ● ● · · · · · · · · · · ·

TIP: Don't Complicate It

This can be a simple practice yet some will complicate it. Don't!

If I offer to scratch your back in exchange for scratching mine, (and gain acceptance, decline, or counter) I've participated in the daily habit

THE AMBITIOUS PROFESSIONAL'S GUIDE TO SURPLUS

Notes

MONTH 8 | 2017 THEME OF THE YEAR: MONEY

Achievement Award Badges

MONTH 9 | 2018 THEME OF THE YEAR: CAREER

- CHAPTER FOURTEEN -
MONTH 9

"Your brand is what other people say about you when you're not in the room"
Jeff Bezos

2018 Theme of The Year: Career

Career is how we are known for the help and value we offer to a specific ecology.

THE AMBITIOUS PROFESSIONAL'S GUIDE TO SURPLUS

Our Marketplace Identity

A linguistic Condition of Life; Career is the state or condition of our public identity; the ability and capacity to help; how we are known for what we do with our mind and our body.

Career is our marketplace identity. It is how we are identified as an offer of help and value in the marketplace. Career is, in general, is how we are known as an identity of value and help in our public world. To build an identity in the public world is to produce more than just a reputation of certain virtues, personal characteristics, or competence in some domain of action, rather, one must be known by a specific group of people for consistently delivering valuable help.

In what ecology do you need to expand or maintain your identity of value/help?

If you expanded or maintained your identity of value/help in this Career Ecology, what Conditions of Life might it improve?

MONTH 9 | 2018 THEME OF THE YEAR: CAREER

The Condition of Your Career

You have a career identity in every ecology - you are known for varying degrees of value/help, ranging from unknown to celebrated.

Unknown: no identity of value, help, or harm

Somewhat Known: a minority of that ecology know or have heard of you as value, help, or harm

Known: a majority of that ecology know or have heard of you as value, help, or harm

Well Known: your identity is a representation of the character of that ecology

Celebrated/Notorious: the ecology identity is a constitutive element of your personal identity; the embodiment and representation of the character of that ecology

The point is not that you are known (for it's own sake), but that you are known for an identity of specific and valuable help,

THE AMBITIOUS PROFESSIONAL'S GUIDE TO SURPLUS

Group Work

With a study group,
discuss how you might elevate your career in a specific ecology. In other words, where would a well-known identity make an impact to your Conditions of Life? Be prepared to challenge yourself and others to think accurately.

1. What is the specific ecology?
2. What is your help to this ecology?
3. What strategies might you deploy?
4. What tactics can you describe?
5. How might you implement this?

_____
_____
_____
_____
_____

MONTH 9 | 2018 THEME OF THE YEAR: CAREER

THE AMBITIOUS PROFESSIONAL'S GUIDE TO SURPLUS

Notes

MONTH 9 | 2018 THEME OF THE YEAR: CAREER

Achievement Award Badges

BEFRIEND BOREDOM

- CHAPTER FIFTEEN -
THE FOURTH THRESHOLD

BEFRIEND BOREDOM

THE AMBITIOUS PROFESSIONAL'S GUIDE TO SURPLUS

Boredom Begets Surplus

You may not enjoy this chapter. Rather than exciting, you may find it, well, boring. However, for those who heed our suggestion, you might, in fact, discover surplus - the point of this guide.

If you read The Millionaire Next Door: The Surprising Secrets of America's Wealthy by Thomas J. Stanley and William D. Danko, their research shows that high-income white-collar professionals are more likely to devote their income to luxury goods or status items, thus neglecting savings and investments.

Most of the millionaire households they profiled did not have the extravagant lifestyles that most people would assume. This finding is backed up by surveys indicating how little these millionaire households have spent on such things as cars, watches, clothing, and other luxury products/services. Most importantly, the book gives a list of reasons why these people managed to accumulate so much wealth (the top one being that "They live below their means").

Well, that does sound boring (but certain, free, consistent, and secure).

While this book does address financial surplus, we want to include surplus in many Conditions of Life. We do not advocate monetary surplus at the cost of satisfaction in other Conditions. Whole-life satisfaction requires that we address all Conditions of Life.

BEFRIEND BOREDOM

Gateway Concerns

Some people focus solely on one Condition of Life at the cost of others. These are Conditions that are naively seen as a gateway to all others. While it is common for the gateway concern to be money, it could also be relationship, career, or any other condition. It is rare to see surplus in one condition while the others are dismissed or threatened.

We advise whole-life satisfaction for long-term fulfillment. In fact, satisfaction in many of the Conditions of Life lays the foundation for sustainable surplus.

Why Befriend Boredom?

Imagine losing 20 pounds; our clothes fit better, we feel more confident, our vitality is rocketing. Now it is time for the rarely accomplished feat of maintenance. Why is it rarely accomplished? First, if we've figured out how to gain or lose weight, maintaining it is a new problem. Second, the excitement wains and we mess with our success, so we've got a familiar problem to fix: losing weight. We befriend the problem rather than making peace with boredom.

Similarly, we befriend our familiar problems. These companion hurdles seem to accompany us throughout our lives. What might we do without them tagging along?

We've rarely created transactions or environments for the boredom of maintenance or the boredom of surplus.

Boredom: A New Problem to Befriend

We advise looking beyond the accomplishment of losing weight or making a pile of cash. Instead, the primary aim is to maintain a surplus in each Condition of Life.

With that context in mind, what might it look like to plan for the long-term maintenance of a surplus of money? How about relationship or career?

Take empty-nesting, for example. Many couples struggle to overcome life beyond the child-raising years. It seems the immediate problem of preparing a life for one's children may leave the couple ill-prepared for the boredom of what comes after.

What are our Aims in Surplus?

Perhaps we only aim to accomplish a goal vs aim to live with it long-term. In this context, is there a new wrinkle on the articulation of our aims? Perhaps we can revise them with this in mind.

BEFRIEND BOREDOM

Inventory Our Surplus Aims

For each Condition of Life below, restate your life-long aims **in 7-words or less** as **Surplus Aims** (after the goal accomplishment).

Health _____

_____

Activity _____

_____

Knowing _____

_____

Relationship _____

_____

Career _____

_____

THE AMBITIOUS PROFESSIONAL'S GUIDE TO SURPLUS

Sociality _____

_____

Money _____

_____

Ethics _____

_____

Education _____

_____

Fitness _____

_____

Aesthetics _____

_____

Environment _____

_____

Politics _____

_____

BEFRIEND BOREDOM

Legacy _____

_____

Self-actualization/spirituality _____

_____

_____

MONTH 10 | 2019 THEME OF THE YEAR: AMBITION

- CHAPTER SIXTEEN -
MONTH 10

"Intelligence without ambition is a bird without wings.."
Salvador Dali

2019 Theme of The Year: Ambition

Ambitious State of Mind: Producing consequential transactions that satisfy ambitious aims.

THE AMBITIOUS PROFESSIONAL'S GUIDE TO SURPLUS

An Ambitious State of Mind

Ambitious Adults make plans and move strategically and tactically to satisfy their Conditions of Life.

They make invitations, offers, commitments, and requests and articulate consequences, judgments, assessments, and assertions that—when accepted—give them the best opportunities to satisfy the unavoidable Conditions of Life. They accept the constraints of the environment, do not argue with or deny the biological, linguistic, and transactional facticity of human life—and in fact utilize their specialized knowledge of it to produce consequential
environments that have others comply. They know their limits, liabilities, and assets. Ambitious Adults respond to opportunities.

An Ambitious State of Mind is evoked, acquired, or imposed by a consequential environment constructed for Ambitious Aims.

Evoked = Ancient reactionary
Acquired = Socially adopted
Imposed = Institutional/Cultural Constraints

An Ambitious Aim is intended to satisfy high aspirations and therefore difficult to achieve.

In most cases, where we can't fully articulate the plans, strategies, and tactics to implement we'll merely withstand the current state of that condition...or boldly evidence our naïveté.

An Ambitious Adult recognizes that an Ambitious State of Mind is an environmental phenomenon.

Are we naïve to the consequential environments we must occupy, produce, or maintain to satisfy our aims?

MONTH 10 | 2019 THEME OF THE YEAR: AMBITION

Group Work

With a study group,
share and discuss the following. Be prepared to challenge yourself and others to think accurately.

Remember a time, a most ambitious time; a period of substantial or life-changing activity. This period took you to a new level of performance, ability, or accomplishment.

1. What was that time? What happened?
2. What was the environment required for that growth?
3. Where were you?
4. Who was instrumental in that growth?
5. What does this reveal about what may be missing?

THE AMBITIOUS PROFESSIONAL'S GUIDE TO SURPLUS

Notes

MONTH 10 | 2019 THEME OF THE YEAR: AMBITION

Achievement Award Badges

Influence Ecology | 121

- CHAPTER SEVENTEEN -
MONTH 11

"Don't get so busy making a living that you forget to make a life."
Dolly Parton

2020 Theme of The Year: Satisfaction

It will do.

THE AMBITIOUS PROFESSIONAL'S GUIDE TO SURPLUS

Inventory Your Ten-Year Aims

For each Condition of Life below, state your aim **in 7-words or less**. State these as **ten-year aims** for each condition.

My age in 10 years _____

Health _____

_____

Activity _____

_____

Knowing _____

_____

Relationship _____

_____

Career _____

_____

MONTH 11 | 2020 THEME OF THE YEAR: SATISFACTION

Sociality _____

_____

Money _____

_____

Ethics _____

_____

Education _____

_____

Fitness _____

_____

Aesthetics _____

_____

Environment _____

_____

Politics _____

_____

THE AMBITIOUS PROFESSIONAL'S GUIDE TO SURPLUS

Legacy _____

_____

Self-actualization/spirituality _____

_____

_____

Why Ten-Year Aims?

Where satisfaction is concerned, it is useful and valuable to address aims with a 10-year time horizon. Stating your age in 10 years makes this all the more real.

MONTH 11 | 2020 THEME OF THE YEAR: SATISFACTION

Notes

THE AMBITIOUS PROFESSIONAL'S GUIDE TO SURPLUS

MONTH 11 | 2020 THEME OF THE YEAR: SATISFACTION

Achievement Award Badges

MONTH 12 | 2021 THEME OF THE YEAR: SURPLUS

- CHAPTER EIGHTEEN -
MONTH 12

"The way to become rich is to put all your eggs in one basket and then watch that basket."
Andrew Carnegie

2021 Theme of The Year: Surplus

It will do.

THE AMBITIOUS PROFESSIONAL'S GUIDE TO SURPLUS

What did you discover on this journey?

MONTH 12 | 2021 THEME OF THE YEAR: SURPLUS

Achievement Award Badges

THE AMBITIOUS PROFESSIONAL'S GUIDE TO SURPLUS

About Influence Ecology

Influence Ecology is a global business curriculum that teaches ambitious professionals how to transact to satisfy their work, career and financial aims.

We teach ambitious business professionals how to construct the fundamental transactions that accelerate their results. Our practical and rigorous study programs help you face the behaviors, practices, and naiveté that keep you from satisfying your work, career, and financial aims.

To satisfy these conditions you must transact.

Guest-level access is available to test drive our programs. During this time you'll gain access to our interactive webinars, online learning system, and private mentorship. Participation is by application only. Successful participants earn candidacy into our advanced program levels. Our members are an international assembly of accomplished professionals, program leaders, and peers from a variety of countries, industries, and cultures.

www.influenceecology.com

www.ingramcontent.com/pod-product-compliance
Lightning Source LLC
Chambersburg PA
CBHW021409290426
44108CB00010B/457